ORGANIZE YOUR LIFE

How to Find Clarity From Within

CHRISTINA RENZELLI

Copyright © 2020 by Christina Renzelli.

No part of this book may be reproduced, transmitted in any form, or stored in a retrieval system or by any means, photocopying, recording, electronic, mechanical or otherwise without prior written permission of the publisher.

The publisher and author do not assume any responsibility for errors, omissions, inaccuracies, inconsistencies or contrary interpretation of this information. Any slights of people, places or organizations are unintentional. Therefore, this product should be used only as a general guide. The purchaser of this publication assumes full responsibility for the use of these materials and information.

Edited by: Sarah Samuel

ISBN: 979-8-6453816-4-6

United States

Contact the Author: http://ChristinaRenzelli.com

First edition, first printing.

DEDICATION

This book is dedicated to my amazing clients,
as a tool to help you tap into your intuition.

TABLE OF CONTENTS

Introduction 1

My story 3

How to Use This Book 7

Phase 1. Clarity & Self-Awareness 9

Phase 2. The Big Declutter: Identify the Blocks & Barriers 15

Phase 3. Saying No. Removing the Barriers, Blocks & Clutter 21

Phase 4. Deeper Reflection 25

Phase 5. The Courageous First Step 33

A Simple Roadmap For Any Area Of Your Life 35

Conclusion 41

Workbook 43

Your Lists 69

More Roadmaps 173

About The Author 181

INTRODUCTION

This book is for you. We have all, at times, felt stuck and overwhelmed, or even bored with our current situations. Yet it is often the case that in these times, life was whispering that there was something more in store for us. If this is you now, if you are ready to stop living in survival mode and start thriving, this simple guide may be the best starter plan to get you moving in the direction of a total life transformation.

The truth is, we are all born for greatness. We all have a great and unique purpose in our lives and feeling dissatisfied, stuck, and overwhelmed are just life's way of telling us that it is time to redirect to something better – something meaningful and brave, where we can make a difference in the lives of others and make a ripple effect of contribution during our short time on Earth.

This book is for you if:

- You feel you have an inspiring mission or purpose to create and you may or may not be clear about what that is yet.

- You intend to make an impact on the world and make a difference in the lives of others: you are a Ripple Effector.

- You value fun and want to live a life of love and joy without taking everything so seriously and making it all so heavy.

- You have a challenge that you are facing and you would like some guidance.

- You are committed to the journey because you know that life is meant to be an adventure.

- You may feel overwhelmed or stuck in your current situation.

- You may have clutter in your home or life.

- You may feel short on time, money, or energy.

- You want to achieve something more.

This book is short and sweet because I do not want you to get lost in unnecessary words or information. We are going to keep it brief, but if you follow the program, you will need to go deep. Self-Awareness is the secret key to success in anything, and this guide will provide you with some tools to start developing skills for self-awareness. Before we get started, I will tell you my story and why I wrote this book.

MY STORY

"Your heart knows the way. Run in that direction." -Rumi

I have always been a teacher and a coach. I started my career as an English language teacher in a small Italian beachside town, where my first job was as the onsite English teacher for the employees of a factory. I loved teaching, but what I secretly loved even more was when I was on my breaks inside my empty classroom and I'd get a knock at the door. One of my students would inevitably be on the other side with some life dilemma or issue that they would want me to help them solve. I LOVED it. It was especially fun because I was much younger than all of my students, still a kid really, at age 22. They were all much older than me; my youngest student was only 24. Italian was not my first language, but that didn't matter. I listened, and together we worked out a plan to figure out a solution to their problem.

Later, I became an elementary school teacher, mostly teaching the third grade. It was my dream job. I loved waking up every morning and coming to school to spend the day with my students. I learned as much (or more) from them as they did from me. Looking back, I can see that my teaching approach was actually a coaching approach. Every student was a magnificent soul on the journey of their lifetime and I felt honored and blessed to be walking by their side during our time together.

A couple of years into my elementary school career, my mom got sick. She fought and battled, and I was by her side every day after the school day ended. I was blessed to have that time with her. After about seven years of teaching, I started to feel the whispers of dissatisfaction with my job. I always loved my students, but something was telling me that I wouldn't be happy doing the exact same thing for the rest of my life. Teaching can be exhausting and stressful; it's not easy taking care of so many people every day. I now recognize this as the beginning stages of burnout. For me, I wasn't dissatisfied because of too much stress or overwhelm, but I felt like I was at the end of the chapter and had another purpose somewhere else, doing something different.

I still loved my work and I didn't feel like I could change careers at that point. Making a change felt too overwhelming, so I became an expert at TOLERATING.

In 2013, my mother passed away after a long, brave fight. In the moment that her soul left her body, I witnessed how precious and temporary life is and I knew that I had to make a change. We only get one chance to live the life that we want, and nothing made that clearer than to see my mother's life pass away. In that moment, I understood in my soul that life is too precious to simply tolerate it when we have the choice to be living it passionately in whatever way we want. **Time is our most precious resource, and I vowed to never waste mine again.** I was never the same after that day. I did have to go back to school, but I made a promise to myself and to my students that I would figure out a way to do work that made my heart feel like it felt during those first years of teaching.

No more tolerating. No more survival mode. No more being stuck. I had one life and I wanted to live it on my terms.

After doing my best to regain my spark for teaching, I finally listened to my heart and quit my teaching job. I still didn't know exactly what I wanted to do. I had some vague sense that I wanted to help people get unstuck. I knew that this was probably called "life coaching" but I wasn't yet 100% comfortable with calling myself a life coach. During a particularly bad period of feeling stuck, I felt compelled to watch the show Hoarders on TV. I think that seeing people who were so physically stuck that their possessions were actually imprisoning them in their homes mirrored the stuck feeling I was experiencing in my life. I didn't have a hoarding issue, but clearing my physical space seemed like an easy thing to start with. I began decluttering all of my possessions that no longer served me. Surprisingly, I felt freer and lighter. One friend even commented that my apartment looked like I was packing up and getting ready to move to Paris. And that was how I felt. Decluttering my possessions helped me feel like I was getting ready for a fresh start, ready for a new adventure phase of my life.

That was how I went from teaching to Professional Organizing. It was a perfect transition because great teachers have to develop great organizational and productivity skills. I named my organizing business Clarity Methods, because my goal was to help others get unstuck and find clarity in their lives. It was a successful business, but soon I started feeling the familiar signs of dread and discontent. But this time, instead of feeling stuck and ignoring the signals, I understood that they were there to tell me it was time to redirect. My organizing clients were not hiring me to get to the root of their problems. Instead, they were hiring me to clean their houses, and that did not feel aligned with what I felt called to do. I wanted to help people get clarity in a more holistic way, to help them organize not just their homes, but their minds. At this point, I had already begun taking coaching classes and I knew that was the right path for me.

Now I work as a life coach, business coach, leadership coach, and teacher coach. I work with wonderful people who know they have something inside of them that is ready to come out and be shared with the world in ways that benefit us all.

I wrote this book for all of those who feel the whispers that they are meant to do something different in their lives, for those who have a clear vision, and for those who are still not exactly sure what their vision is yet. Sometimes the hardest part of the journey is figuring out what you really want. That's why I named my organizing business Clarity Methods. I wrote this book to help you find clarity. Let's get started.

HOW TO USE THIS BOOK

This book is what I call "A Starter Guide." It's a simple blueprint to help you:

- Organize your mind

- Use writing and list making to organize your thoughts, ideas, and desires

- Start identifying what you don't want, so you can declutter it from your life

- Identify what you do want

- Figure out what steps you need to take to get started on the journey of making your dream a reality

- Identify energy wasters and obstacles that are keeping you stuck

- Start taking steps to create your ideal life

I originally created a model of this method when I was a professional organizer. I used the method to help my clients gain clarity in two important areas: what their dream scenario was and what was blocking them from it. The blocks were listed as mostly physical clutter. But I believe that physical clutter can represent something deeper. Often it is the symptom of emotional clutter or other forms of wasted energy. This guide can help you "unscramble" most situations, including relationship problems, an overbooked calendar, or problems finding the right clients for your business.

My purpose for writing this book is to support you in finding and developing your own self-awareness. **Self-awareness is the secret key to success in every area of life.**

You will most likely read through it in less than a day, or even one hour. It is designed to be a quick read. However, the writing exercises are meant to be done at your own pace and will take some time.

You may relate to some parts more than others, and it's okay if some parts do not feel compelling to you.

Have fun with it. Afterall, you are creating a new life for yourself. Enjoy.

PHASE 1. CLARITY & SELF-AWARENESS

For any goal, mission or dream to become reality, we have to start with a clear vision. Many of us are stuck in the phase of trying to figure out what we want. Often this is because:

- We have what we thought we wanted, but it isn't really satisfying.

- We are plateaued, and what we worked so hard to reach feels like just a plateau, not the peak of the mountain.

- We checked all the boxes of what someone (society, family, partner, manager) told us they SHOULD want, but it is not fulfilling our soul's desire.

- We have a belief system that told us to work hard, struggle, and tolerate, so we have long been doing this on autopilot without stopping to notice that it's not what we wanted at all.

- We are so overwhelmed and living in survival mode that we fear there is no hope to ever rise above a life we merely "get through." We dread Monday, survive to Wednesday, then survive again to Friday at which point we numb, dread Monday, and repeat.

- We have gotten so out of touch with even the possibility of dreaming or creating a vision for our lives that we are simply afraid to want something different.

- Our lives are filled with so much mental or physical clutter that it is overwhelming and blocking us from hearing what our hearts really want.

From my experience, the hardest part of getting what you want is figuring out what you want. Our lives have become so cluttered with junk that our inner guiding voice, our intuition, gets muddled and drowned out by all the noise. We begin to doubt our intuition and replace it with the "status quo" or the word of some "authority" who claims to know what's best for us. Figuring out what you want is often the longest phase. After you get really clear about exactly what you want, you can work out the plan to make it happen.

I have met too many people who waste their precious time and energy chasing dreams that aren't really theirs because they weren't able to slow down enough to ask themselves what they really want.

Those who live their dream lives are clear about what they want, and what they don't want.

To get clear about what you want, start by identifying and DECLUTTERING all that you DON'T want.

Exercise: Get clearer about what you want by identifying what you DON'T want:

Area of Life:_____

I don't want:	Why?	I do want:	Why?

This exercise seems overly simplistic, but it powerfully shows some of the blind spots surrounding what we tolerate. I have one client who used it to clarify what she wanted in a relationship. She was getting burned out on the dating scene because she was wasting too much time and energy going out with people that were not the right matches for her. By using this simple organizer, we were able to clarify the qualities she was looking for by first identifying the qualities she did not want to tolerate. It simplified the process and she is now dating someone with all the qualities she wanted in a partner.

Her example:

I don't want:	Why?	I do want:	Why?
Shallow, overly superficial	Boring, uninteresting	Kind, deep	Can have deeper, more interesting conversations
workaholic	Won't have time to get to know each other	Balanced work and free time	We can spend time and get to know each other

This chart can be used for any area of life. Some examples include:

Job, career, business
Relationships/friendships
Home
Calendar/Schedule

It's often difficult to distinguish between a SHOULD and a true WANT. A lot of clutter and wasted energy can come from doing what we think we "should" do.

Shoulds are not our true wants. They are usually someone else's expectations for us: society, family, partner. It's important to get clarity about which things are shoulds in our life, and which are true wants.

Remember this: **SHOULDS OFTEN STEAL ENERGY FROM OUR TRUE WANTS.**

Our time is our most precious resource. When we spend it on what we SHOULD do, rather than investing it in what we WANT to do, we waste it and we never get it back. The result is that we feel drained, lethargic, tired, hollow and hopeless. Take your time to reflect on your "shoulds", and then be brave enough to start saying NO to them.

I should:	How I feel about it:	I want to:	How I feel about it:

Many people find their first pass at this chart to look like this:

I should:	How I feel about it:	I want to:	How I feel about it:
"should"	Dread/procrastination	"true want"	GUILTY

When we are stuck living a life of shoulds, we are often controlled by a sense of GUILT for wanting what we truly want. This can require some deeper internal investigating with the help of a counselor or coach, because if you are creating the life of your dreams, guilt could be a major roadblock on your journey. Sometimes guilt comes up because we don't want to disappoint others by living a different story than they expect for us. If you feel guilt regarding something that you truly want, ask yourself the following:

Is my "want" hurting/negatively affecting anyone else?
Is my "want" hurting/negatively affecting myself or my life?

If the answers are no, you are probably struggling with "false guilt," which is just the fear of disappointing others or not living up to their expectations, or the fear of being judged.

What are you TOLERATING?

What are you tolerating in your life? Often when someone is living their life in survival mode, they tolerate a lot. This is usually because they don't realize that they have a choice not to tolerate it.

Remember the story I told you at the beginning? I was tolerating a daily routine that was draining my energy instead of making an alternative plan. Change was so difficult to imagine that I truly believed it was impossible. But it wasn't impossible; I had a choice. It took planning, courage, and risk to make the change, but I am happy to say that I am no longer tolerating a daily routine that drains my energy.

We tolerate a lot more than we realize, simply because we are used to it. Life doesn't have to be like a prison. You are not a prisoner. You have the choice to live a life of purpose.

List everything you are tolerating and come up with at least one other option that you would enjoy more:

I'm tolerating:	Because:	Another option is:

"Your task is not to seek for love, but merely to seek and find all the barriers within yourself that you have built against it." -RUMI

PHASE 2. THE BIG DECLUTTER: IDENTIFY THE BLOCKS & BARRIERS

Now that you see we have to declutter before we can organize, I want to talk a little about invisible forms of clutter that infiltrate many of our lives. You might recognize some of them from the exercises above. This clutter appears in the form of:

Guilt

Guilt is tricky because it's usually false. False guilt is feeling guilty when you haven't done anything wrong, and you have not violated your own values. True guilt is felt when you violate your own values. I work with many "people pleasers" and "recovering people pleasers" and I find that guilt often steers their ship. They don't do what they really want because they are afraid that they might disappoint someone they love or work with. This is a problem because they end up disappointing themselves instead and their life becomes one major disappointment after another. It doesn't have to be this way.

Shame

Shame is a horrible joy thief. It basically tells us that there is something wrong with us that no other human has experienced or would understand and that we should hide it from the world. When you realize that you are a perfectly imperfect human like everyone else, you can let that shame go and it will no longer block you from spreading love and light in the world.

Shoulds

Shoulds are simply someone else's expectations for our life: Society, family, partner, manager, etc. We fill our to-do lists with shoulds, giving them a lot of attention, but shoulds muddle up our true wants and often upon examination, we can see that they are simply energy wasters that block us from living lives of meaning and true purpose.

Unprocessed Trauma

Our brains are designed to protect us from danger. This means that we experience a stress response when the brain recognizes something associated with past trauma or anything that is unfamiliar and out of our control.

When trauma is unprocessed, we tend to avoid it at all costs. This avoidance then gets in the way of our lives. We are not free when we have to avoid certain situations or associations.

People Pleasing

Many of us have let people pleasing rule our lives while we stay in the back seat just letting others make decisions for us. But as Harriet B. Braiker, Ph.D. writes in her brilliant book *The Disease to Please*, "Unless you act to stop this dangerous cycle of pleasing others at the expense of yourself, you will eventually hit the proverbial wall. Your energy will be exhausted..." People pleasing can come up in many forms such as:

- saying yes when we really want to say no
- avoiding conflict or not sticking up for ourselves
- always being available
- being "flexible"
- being afraid of saying what you really want
- being afraid of "rocking the boat" especially when you admire someone and want them to like you, which leads to the next block...

Approval Seeking

Approval seeking takes some of the same forms as people pleasing. Approval seeking happens when we want to impress others or make a good impression. It sometimes shows up when we are afraid to make mistakes or be a beginner at something new. We often don't put ourselves out there because we don't want to appear unpolished or imperfect. Approval seeking is a form of perfectionism. People often leave their potential locked inside of them because they are so afraid that someone may not approve, that they don't want to take the risk of succeeding. I once knew an excellent public speaker who delayed getting on stage for years because she was afraid of being a beginner and afraid of being judged as less than perfect. The truth is, people don't care if you're perfect. They care that you are human and that you are doing whatever you are doing with heart. They care that you can help them and make a difference. It's that simple.

Being Nice Rather than Kind: The Confusion and the Truth

It is my opinion that being NICE is very different than being KIND. Nice is: surface, people pleasing, appearances rather than authentic, polite. It is very social. Nice is when you go out on a first date and tell someone you had a good time, but the truth is you didn't. Nice is getting someone's hopes up because you are afraid to tell the truth. Nice is when a teacher glosses over a mistake or gives an easy A. Kind is very different. Kind is honest. Kind means that you take the risk of disappointing someone when the truth may hurt. Kind is when you go on a first date and at the end you tell the truth that you weren't feeling a connection. Kind is when a teacher firmly yet respectfully redirects a student when they make a mistake. Kind is courageous, while nice is cowardly.

Where in your life are you being "nice?"

I am "nice when...	It would be kinder to instead...

Weak Boundaries/Lack of Boundaries

Not all of us were taught that we have the right to boundaries in our lives. Many of us were raised to believe that we should be on call for anyone who needs anything from us: our time, our money, our energy, our space. Lack of boundaries may be one of the most common and most energy draining blocks that I see among my clients. The problem with having weak boundaries is this: You spend all of your energy on EVERYONE ELSE and then there's none left over for YOURSELF. This is a formula for disaster, burnout, and living a life that's not your own. The only real way to serve others is to identify and set yourself some strong boundaries, regain and maintain your energy, and then give it to those you choose to give it to.

Fear of the Unfamiliar

Fear of the unfamiliar is common for all humans with a brainstem. Our brains are designed to keep us alive; they are designed for survival. Anything unfamiliar is perceived as a threat by the brainstem and this sends us into the stress response: fight, flight, freeze, flock. When you learn that this is a natural, normal, human protection mechanism, you can learn strategies to override the system, strategies to self regulate. So when you see that all of your blocks are associated with fearing the unfamiliar, you can breath a deep sigh of relief and know that you are human, it's normal, and there are ways to override this.

Planning for Scarcity Rather than Abundance

The truth is, we get what we plan for and many of us are used to planning for scarcity. Instead of planning for all the abundance, joy and love we can have in our lives, we plan for disasters, problems, and lack. Going around thinking about how you aren't going to have enough usually means you won't have enough. Just try this: Notice when you plan for negative circumstances rather than expect positive ones. It will shift your whole life if you start to notice it. Notice it. And then start planning for abundance instead. It really works.

Self-Doubt/Underestimating Your Own Potential

Self-doubt simply prevents us from trying. We think we aren't good enough or don't have enough knowledge or skill or experience, so we don't bother trying. Millions of us are walking around, barely surviving our lives, when instead we have all this untapped potential inside of us. Self-doubt is a real killer. It's dangerous. Think of all the things you could do if you just gave it your best shot. You would amaze yourself.

Fear of Conflict

The fear of conflict makes people tolerate all kinds of stuff that they don't really have to and it keeps us from connecting with one another on a deeper level. I see this as a major block in so many relationships. When we fear conflict, we are really fearing the truth. We are afraid that the truth of our wants or our situation will be rejected and disapproved of by the other person. The good news is that conflict can be the gateway to connection. Sometimes when we just put it all out on the table, true and deep connection can occur.

Fear of Failure

I don't know many people who WANT to fail. The fear of failure is pretty common, and the only real remedy I've found is actual failure. I used to fear failure, until one day I had a terrible "flop." (Well, I had two). I was giving an impromptu speech. I could have prepared better, but I decided I knew what I needed to say and didn't prepare. On stage I completely choked up. It was embarrassing. I wanted to run away. But then something magical happened: I didn't die. Nobody really cared. They just forgot about me and moved on with their lives. I didn't hurt anyone with my terrible performance, I just bruised my own ego. After that, I got braver. Of course, I'd failed at other things before that and have also failed since then, but it sticks out in my mind as the day my biggest fear didn't really hurt me as much as I thought it would.

Believing You Don't Have a Choice

So many people live their lives assuming that they don't get to choose the direction of their lives. Sure, there are certain things that happen that we don't have a choice in, but not nearly as many as I used to believe. We really are much freer to choose than we realize most of the time. You are the captain of this ship.

For example, I believed I didn't have the choice to make a career change. The truth was, I did have a choice, but it was not easy or comfortable to make. It required me to give up the perceived safety of living with what was familiar and take the risk of leaping into the unknown. Sometimes the choices are so uncomfortable that we just settle into the belief that we don't have any at all.

Habits

Habits and routines can make or break us. The problem is obvious when our habits are blocking us from what we want, but the real danger is when we aren't AWARE that we have bad habits.

Patterns

Patterns are the situations we continually find ourselves in or the reactions we consistently find ourselves having to outside circumstances. For example, I have a friend who always dates people who don't have enough money to support themselves. They then start to depend on my friend to foot the bill. This is a pattern in my friend's relationship history. The good news is, my friend has identified it and is doing the work inside to change the pattern through awareness and practice.

Beliefs

Our beliefs are more powerful than we may ever realize. They have been influenced by everything in our lives since we were born. They are formed by our parents' beliefs, their parents' beliefs, society, trauma, and love. We have all formed our beliefs as the story of our lives, and sometimes these beliefs do not serve us in living the life of our dreams. Sometimes the beliefs are major roadblocks. I once knew a woman who believed she was ugly. Bullying during her adolescence combined with some other traumas had left her feeling diminished and ugly. She lived with the shame for years, not understanding that it was not true and even a major block to living her true purpose.

PHASE 3. SAYING NO. REMOVING THE BARRIERS, BLOCKS & CLUTTER

This may be the hardest phase of the plan because now you have to stop doing the things that you've been doing forever. You have to say no to the things you've said yes to and allowed for so long before you realized it was draining the life out of you. It's hard, but you can do it.

It takes PRACTICE.

Remember, this is a process and we are not after perfection. We are about growth, transformation, and learning, and the only way that happens is through PRACTICE.

At first, when you try something new, it feels clunky. It's uncomfortable and you'll feel like you're doing it wrong or making mistakes. You might feel like you're failing. But guess what? That's all part of the process.

FAILURES, FLOPS AND MISTAKES ARE RICH OPPORTUNITIES TO LEARN AND GROW

Any time one of my coaching clients has a big failure, we celebrate and then we dissect it to find out what the lesson is. I am a firm believer that mistakes are simply lessons in disguise. They are all part of the transformation process.

Say No

Now you have to decide what you are no longer going to allow into your precious life. This can be very emotional, especially when related to behaviors from the people you love.

This doesn't mean that you need to stop associating with someone you love, but it means identifying and possibly saying no to the behaviors that you may have been unjustly tolerating.

I'm now saying NO to:	This may be hard because:	It's best for me because:

Another way of saying this is:

I'm decluttering from my life:	Resistance I am feeling:	Reward from decluttering:

PHASE 4. DEEPER REFLECTION

By this phase, you may be much clearer about what you don't want to keep tolerating in your life. You will most likely be feeling much freer, and it may be easier to see the vision of what you want for your life. In Phase 5, we will talk about creating a roadmap for taking the first steps toward achieving your goal. If you are still unclear or if you want to deepen your self-awareness skills, play around with some of the lists in this section. I began compiling this List of Lists years ago as an idea for my coaching clients to dig deeper into the stories of their lives. Now I'm seeing that list making can be a powerful self-reflection tool. Choose the ones that seem interesting to you and dive deep. The lists can be used as self-reflection tools or ways to get to know other people on a deeper level.

This is just an overview of the Lists of Lists. At the end of this book, there will be a page for each list where you can list your own answers to the questions.

List of Lists

- List of everything your heart desires:

- Imagine you are 100 years old. You're looking back on your life, having experienced everything you'd ever dreamed of. What are you grateful for?

- List of fears. List each fear and why it scares you:

- List of all the people you love. Describe what you love about them if you can:

- List of all the people who have ever broken your heart and what you learned from them.

- List of all your true friends:

- List of regrets:

- List of things you would regret from your deathbed (let these be your reasons to stop tolerating and start choosing the life you want!):

- List of all your rejections (that you have been rejected by/from):

- List of everything you're afraid to be rejected from:

- List of times you got rejected and what you learned from each moment. What were the blessings that you can see in hindsight?

- List of past failures:

- List of current failures:

- List of things you're afraid of failing at:

- List of flops and failures, and how they redirected you:

- List of all the places you want to visit:

- List of twists of fate (example: If I hadn't been rejected by my dream grad school, I would never have moved to Italy):

- List of everything you want to learn:

- List of favorite songs and why:

- List of favorite relatives:

- List of best teachers, in school and in life:

- List of best memories:

- List all the things you know how to do that would be valuable to teach others:

- List goals that you keep meaning to accomplish but still haven't gotten around to (are they "shoulds"?):

- List of things your intuition told you but you chose to ignore:

- List of mistakes:

- List of ways you've wasted time.

- List of ways you've wasted money.

- List of ways you've wasted energy:

- List of things you're proud of:

- List of things you love about yourself:

- List of things you want to change about yourself. Why? Now try seeing those things with love and acceptance:

- List of what you're grateful for:

- List of things you wish you could tell someone but feel you can't:

- List of your darkest secrets:

- List of special talents and skills you have that others would pay you for:

- List of things you put off doing but would do if you had someone to help you:

- List of descriptors you hope to be included in your obituary:

- List of things you wish you had appreciated long ago:

- List of things that ended too soon:

- List of reasons you care what others think of you:

- List of things you would do if you didn't care what anybody else thought:

- List of things you'd do if you had more time:

- List of brilliant ideas that you haven't brought to fruition yet:

- List of everything you want more of:

- List of everything you want less of:

- List of all the things you believe you have no choice about:

- List of all the things you do have a choice about:

- List of everything you believe to be the truth about love:

- List of everything you believe to be the truth about money:

- List of everything you want for yourself in life:

- List of all the things you can let go of for a better life:

- List of all your disappointments:

- List of all the things that energize you:

- List of all the people who energize you:

- List of all the things that drain your energy:

- List of all the people who drain your energy:

- List of everything you'd do with $1,000,000.00 extra right now:

- List of all the things you gave up on because it seemed too hard:

- List of everything you wish was easier:

- List of all the things you WISH you loved about yourself:

- List of all the things about yourself that you feel critical or ashamed of:

- List what makes you feel attractive:

- List what makes you feel unattractive:

- List what makes you feel strong:

- List what makes you feel weak:

- List the ways you have made a positive difference in someone else's life:

- List the ways you have made a negative difference in someone else's life:

- List the people who have made a positive difference in your life:

- List the people who have made a negative difference in your life. What can you learn from the experience?

- List of all the ways you feel or have felt stuck:

- List of all the things you wish you could say no to:

- List of everything that feels like an obligation. Are you really obligated? Why?

- List of all the things you wish you could say yes to:

- List of all the topics you would write about if you were writing books:

- List of all the jobs you would work if every job paid the same:

- List of all the things you'd do if you had more time:

- List all the things you would do with one year of paid vacation:

- List of all the things you need the most in this moment:

- List of all the things you want the most in this moment:

- List of all the beauty you've witnessed today:

- List of everything you are good at and everything you are BEST at:

- List the things people ask your help for:

- List everything you enjoy doing on a day-to-day basis:

- List of the things you do that you do NOT enjoy:

- List of all the things you want to quit:

- List of all the things you want to start:

- List of all the things you want to finish:

- List everything and everyone you are avoiding in your life:

- List all the lies you tell yourself/beliefs about yourself that are holding you back:

- List the lies you tell others:

- List your excuses for not living your dreams:

- List everything that you have left undecided:

- List of everything you would create if you had a magic wand:

- List everything you would make disappear if you had a magic wand:

- List of everything you would change if you had a magic wand:

- List of all your dreams:

- List of all your fears:

- List of everything you are going to do to start making your dreams a reality:

PHASE 5. THE COURAGEOUS FIRST STEP

There are many reasons that people are afraid to take the first step into their dream life. I think that oftentimes, they have made some small, unsupported attempts in the past, hit a roadblock or mini-failure, and then retreated back to the safety of their comfortable zone of discontent. I think that the main reason is this:

The unknown is scary! Our brains are designed to fear the unknown. The minute we sense unfamiliarity, our brains send us fleeing back to safety. One way to counteract this is to tiptoe into the unfamiliar, new territory. I have worked with countless clients who get excited about their big goals and plan to dive straight in with everything they've got. This happens a lot around the New Year with giant fitness goals. These big goals usually fail because our brainstems get overloaded with too much newness. The key is: SMALL CHANGES ADD UP. This works especially well with physical goals, such as fitness. When you go from walking ten steps a day to an hour long HIIT routine, it can feel like torture, and the body will do everything it can to protect itself from that torture. However, if you go from walking ten steps a day to walking 100 steps a day, the body can ease into it.

This works for most goals. Let's say you want to write a book, but you never write at all. Start with the smallest goal possible. For example, write one paragraph per day in your journal.

I have found that this also counteracts RESISTANCE, which is something we should all be aware of when trying to make a big change. Resistance happens when your ego tries to push you back into your old patterns of safety. It's doing its job, trying to keep you safely in the zone of dissatisfaction because the zone of dissatisfaction is safe. You are in survival mode. The ego is meant to keep you surviving, as is the brainstem. But you don't want to survive, just like you don't want to tolerate. You want to THRIVE.

A SIMPLE ROADMAP FOR ANY AREA OF YOUR LIFE

In this chapter, I am introducing you to a simple roadmap you can use for one or more areas of your life. You can revisit this section time and time again as you begin upgrading your life and accomplishing your goals and dreams.

I have included additional roadmaps you can use in Part 2: The Workbook, in the second half of this book. Take your time and connect inside as you answer these questions:

1. Choose an area of your life to "upgrade:"

_____

_____

_____

2. What does it look like now?

_____

_____

_____

3. What is my dream scenario?

_____

_____

_____

4. Figure out the difference between your current situation and your ideal situation:

Now: (describe in detail)	Ideal: (describe in detail)

5. From the current situation, what am I tolerating that I do not want?

_____

_____

_____

_____

6. What are your identified BLOCKS that are keeping you stuck and away from your ideal situation? Blocks can be habits, patterns, and beliefs we didn't realize we had but aren't helpful.

Identified Blocks	Why have I tolerated this?

7. What are the blocks I'm ready to consider removing? Note that there are always some benefits to keeping blocks. Be aware of the benefits as well as the benefits of letting them go.

Identified Block:	Fear I have about letting it go:	Benefit of keeping this block:	Benefit of letting go of this block:

8. What are the blocks I'm deciding to let go of and how am I going to do that?

Blocks I am DECIDING to let go:	This looks like: (my plan)

BUILDING THE IDEAL SITUATION:

1. Have the blocks been identified (and removed)?

---

2. Be very clear about what you want and what you don't want. Again, your ideal scenario needs to be super clear:

Don't Want:	Want:

Make sure there are no SHOULDS involved:

I Should:	Makes me feel:	What I really want:	How I feel about my want:

3. Do you feel clear about what you want now?

_____

4. Does your want feel possible?

_____

If yes, go to #5 below.

If no, why doesn't it feel possible?

_____

_____

_____

You may have some beliefs that are left over and creating a block. They need to be examined and removed. Seek a friend or coach to discuss and get to the root.

5. Congratulations! You are ready to create your ideal scenario.

What is the first step toward this ideal scenario that you are going to take? Make it something manageable, simple and doable. Make it something you can do with joy, NOT something heavy or punishing.

_____

_____

_____

_____

6. Who can support you in this process?

_____

Remember, all new endeavors are unfamiliar, and our subconscious perceives "unfamiliar" as a threat. The only way to counteract this is small, steady steps in the right direction and PRACTICE.

It takes PRACTICE and REPETITION to learn and transform and create a new reality for yourself.

Be on the lookout for:

Your old patterns and tolerations trying to creep back in. It takes a lot of awareness and practice to identify them and say NO to them. They always try to creep back in. Don't worry, this will get easier over time, and your life will feel better and freer without them.

CONCLUSION

I hope that you have enjoyed this starter guide to upgrading your life. My intention is to help spark you into a deeper self-awareness, which is the key to all success in life, love, business and finances. Please use this book as a guide and continue into some deeper journaling exercises. This book can be used for individuals or for groups, and my wish for you is that it guides you to the life of your dreams.

If you would like additional support through individual coaching, group coaching programs, or workshops, please email me at christina@christinarenzelli.com.

WORKBOOK

In this section, you will keep track of your daily focus and insights for 21 days. It has been designed as a workbook/journal for the areas of life that you are seeking clarity. During the 21 days, you can pick one area to focus on, or if you prefer, you can just see what comes up for you each day throughout all areas of your life. You may notice that when you focus on just one area, other parts of your life begin to shift.

The areas identified are:

Home

Relationships

Work

Money

Creativity

Purpose/Making a Difference

Self-Care/Health

Any Additional Area You May Identify in Your Life

You can focus on just one area for all of the 21 days, or if you prefer, you can just see what comes up for you throughout all areas of your life. It depends on what area of life you want to focus on. You may also notice that when you focus on just one area, other parts of your life begin to shift.

Date: _____

Area of Focus: _____

Ways my energy felt drained: _____
_____
_____
_____

Ways my energy felt recharged: _____
_____
_____
_____
_____

Because of this insight, I will _____
_____
_____
_____
_____

I will say no to _____
_____

I will say YES to _____
_____

Date: _____

Area of Focus: _____

Ways my energy felt drained: _____

_____

_____

_____

Ways my energy felt recharged: _____

_____

_____

_____

_____

Because of this insight, I will _____

_____

_____

_____

I will say no to _____

_____

I will say YES to _____

_____

Date: _____

Area of Focus: _____

Ways my energy felt drained: _____
_____
_____
_____

Ways my energy felt recharged: _____
_____
_____
_____
_____

Because of this insight, I will _____
_____
_____
_____
_____

I will say no to _____
_____

I will say YES to _____
_____

Date: _____

Area of Focus: _____

Ways my energy felt drained: _____

_____

_____

_____

Ways my energy felt recharged: _____

_____

_____

_____

_____

Because of this insight, I will _____

_____

_____

_____

_____

I will say no to _____

_____

I will say YES to _____

_____

Date: _____

Area of Focus: _____

Ways my energy felt drained: _____
_____
_____
_____

Ways my energy felt recharged: _____
_____
_____
_____

Because of this insight, I will _____
_____
_____
_____

I will say no to _____
_____

I will say YES to _____
_____

Date: _____

Area of Focus: _____

Ways my energy felt drained: _____
_____
_____
_____

Ways my energy felt recharged: _____
_____
_____
_____
_____

Because of this insight, I will _____
_____
_____
_____
_____

I will say no to _____
_____

I will say YES to _____
_____

Date: _____

Area of Focus: _____

Ways my energy felt drained: _____
_____
_____
_____

Ways my energy felt recharged: _____
_____
_____
_____

Because of this insight, I will _____
_____
_____
_____

I will say no to _____

I will say YES to _____
_____

Date: _____

Area of Focus: _____

Ways my energy felt drained: _____

_____

_____

_____

Ways my energy felt recharged: _____

_____

_____

_____

_____

Because of this insight, I will _____

_____

_____

_____

I will say no to _____

_____

I will say YES to _____

_____

Date: _____

Area of Focus: _____

Ways my energy felt drained: _____

_____

_____

_____

Ways my energy felt recharged: _____

_____

_____

_____

_____

Because of this insight, I will _____

_____

_____

_____

_____

I will say no to _____

_____

I will say YES to _____

_____

Date: _____

Area of Focus: _____

Ways my energy felt drained: _____

_____

_____

_____

Ways my energy felt recharged: _____

_____

_____

_____

_____

Because of this insight, I will _____

_____

_____

_____

_____

I will say no to _____

_____

I will say YES to _____

_____

Date: _____

Area of Focus: _____

Ways my energy felt drained: _____
_____
_____
_____

Ways my energy felt recharged: _____
_____
_____
_____
_____

Because of this insight, I will _____
_____
_____
_____

I will say no to _____
_____

I will say YES to _____
_____

Date: _____

Area of Focus: _____

Ways my energy felt drained: _____
_____
_____
_____

Ways my energy felt recharged: _____
_____
_____
_____
_____

Because of this insight, I will _____
_____
_____
_____
_____

I will say no to _____
_____

I will say YES to _____
_____

Date: _____

Area of Focus: _____

Ways my energy felt drained: _____

_____

_____

_____

Ways my energy felt recharged: _____

_____

_____

_____

Because of this insight, I will _____

_____

_____

_____

I will say no to _____

_____

I will say YES to _____

_____

Date: _____

Area of Focus: _____

Ways my energy felt drained: _____

_____

_____

_____

Ways my energy felt recharged: _____

_____

_____

_____

_____

Because of this insight, I will _____

_____

_____

_____

I will say no to _____

_____

I will say YES to _____

_____

Date: _____

Area of Focus: _____

Ways my energy felt drained: _____
_____
_____
_____

Ways my energy felt recharged: _____
_____
_____
_____
_____

Because of this insight, I will _____
_____
_____
_____
_____

I will say no to _____
_____

I will say YES to _____
_____

Date: _____

Area of Focus: _____

Ways my energy felt drained: _____

_____

_____

_____

Ways my energy felt recharged: _____

_____

_____

_____

_____

Because of this insight, I will _____

_____

_____

_____

I will say no to _____

_____

I will say YES to _____

_____

Date: _____

Area of Focus: _____

Ways my energy felt drained: _____
_____
_____
_____

Ways my energy felt recharged: _____
_____
_____
_____

Because of this insight, I will _____
_____
_____
_____

I will say no to _____
_____

I will say YES to _____
_____

Date: _____

Area of Focus: _____

Ways my energy felt drained: _____

_____

_____

_____

Ways my energy felt recharged: _____

_____

_____

_____

_____

Because of this insight, I will _____

_____

_____

_____

I will say no to _____

_____

I will say YES to _____

_____

Date: _____

Area of Focus: _____

Ways my energy felt drained: _____
_____
_____
_____

Ways my energy felt recharged: _____
_____
_____
_____
_____

Because of this insight, I will _____
_____
_____
_____
_____

I will say no to _____
_____

I will say YES to _____
_____

Date: _____

Area of Focus: _____

Ways my energy felt drained: _____

_____

_____

_____

Ways my energy felt recharged: _____

_____

_____

_____

Because of this insight, I will _____

_____

_____

_____

I will say no to _____

_____

I will say YES to _____

_____

Date: _____

Area of Focus: _____

Ways my energy felt drained: _____

_____

_____

_____

Ways my energy felt recharged: _____

_____

_____

_____

_____

Because of this insight, I will _____

_____

_____

_____

I will say no to _____

_____

I will say YES to _____

_____

Date: _____

Area of Focus: _____

Ways my energy felt drained: _____

_____

_____

_____

Ways my energy felt recharged: _____

_____

_____

_____

_____

Because of this insight, I will _____

_____

_____

_____

I will say no to _____

_____

I will say YES to _____

_____

Date: _____

Area of Focus: _____

Ways my energy felt drained: _____

_____

_____

_____

Ways my energy felt recharged: _____

_____

_____

_____

_____

Because of this insight, I will _____

_____

_____

_____

_____

I will say no to _____

_____

I will say YES to _____

_____

YOUR LISTS

Directions for Lists: Chose any list that seems interesting and write your own list of answers to the questions. Have fun with this exercise.

List of everything your heart desires:

Imagine you are 100 years old. You're looking back on your life, having experienced everything you'd ever dreamed of. What are you grateful for?

_____
_____
_____
_____
_____
_____
_____
_____
_____
_____
_____
_____
_____
_____
_____
_____
_____
_____

List of fears. List everything that you are afraid of and WHY.

List each fear and why it scares you:

Fear: Why it Scares You:

List of all the people you love. Describe why you love them if you can:

List of all the people who have ever broken your heart and what you learned from them.

Heart Breakers & Lessons Learned:

List of all your true friends:

List of regrets:

List of things you would regret from your deathbed (let these be your reasons to stop tolerating and start choosing the life you want!):

_____

_____

_____

_____

_____

_____

_____

_____

_____

_____

_____

_____

_____

_____

_____

_____

_____

List of things you'd feel you had missed out on if you didn't experience them by the end of your life:

___

List of all your rejections (that you have been rejected by/from):

_____
_____
_____
_____
_____
_____
_____
_____
_____
_____
_____
_____
_____
_____
_____
_____
_____
_____
_____
_____
_____

List of everything you're afraid to be rejected from:

List of times you got rejected and what you learned from each moment. What were the blessings that you can see in hindsight?

_____

_____

_____

_____

_____

_____

_____

_____

_____

_____

_____

_____

_____

_____

_____

_____

_____

_____

_____

List of past failures:

List of current failures:

List of things you're afraid of failing at:

List of flops and failures and how they redirected you:

List of all the places you want to visit:

List of twists of fate. (For example: If I hadn't been rejected to grad school, I would never have moved to Italy):

_____
_____
_____
_____
_____
_____
_____
_____
_____
_____
_____
_____
_____
_____
_____
_____
_____
_____

List of everything you want to learn:

List of favorite songs and why:

List of favorite relatives and what makes them special to you:

List of best teachers, in school and in life:

List of best memories:

List of all the things you know how to do that would be valuable to teach others:

List goals that you keep meaning to accomplish but still haven't got around to (are they "shoulds"?):

List of things your intuition told you but you chose to ignore:

_____
_____
_____
_____
_____
_____
_____
_____
_____
_____
_____
_____
_____
_____
_____
_____
_____
_____

List of mistakes:

List of ways you've wasted time.

List of ways you've wasted money.

List of ways you've wasted energy:

List of things you're proud of:

List of things you love about yourself:

List of things you want to change about yourself. Why? Now try seeing those things with love and acceptance:

List of what you're grateful for:

List of things you wish you could tell someone but feel you can't:

List of your darkest secrets:

List of special talents and skills you have that others would pay you for:

List of things you put off doing but would do if you had someone to help you:

List of descriptors you hope to be included in your obituary:

List of things you wish you had appreciated long ago:

List of things that ended too soon:

List of reasons you care what others think of you:

List of things you would do if you didn't care what anybody else thought:

List of things you'd do if you had more time:

_____
_____
_____
_____
_____
_____
_____
_____
_____
_____
_____
_____
_____
_____
_____
_____
_____
_____
_____
_____

List of brilliant ideas that you haven't brought to fruition yet:

List of everything you want more of:

_____
_____
_____
_____
_____
_____
_____
_____
_____
_____
_____
_____
_____
_____
_____
_____
_____
_____
_____
_____

List of everything you want less of:

List of all the things you believe you have no choice about:

List of all the things you do have a choice about:

List of everything you believe to be the truth about love:

List of everything you believe to be the truth about money:

List of everything you want for yourself in life:

List of all the things you can let go of for a better life:

List of all your disappointments:

List of all the things that energize you:

List of all the people who energize you:

List of all the things that drain your energy:

List of all the people who drain your energy:

List of everything you'd do with $1,000,000.00 extra right now:

List of all the things you gave up on because it seemed too hard:

List of everything you wish was easier:

List of all the things you WISH you loved about yourself:

List of all the things about yourself that you feel critical or ashamed of:

List what makes you feel attractive:

List what makes you feel unattractive:

List what makes you feel strong:

List what makes you feel weak:

List the ways you have made a positive difference in someone else's life:

List the ways you have made a negative difference in someone else's life:

List the people who have made a positive difference in your life:

List the people who have made a negative difference in your life. What can you learn from the experience?

List of all the ways you feel or have felt stuck:

List of all the things you wish you could say no to:

List of everything that feels like an obligation. Are you really obligated? Why?

List of all the things you wish you could say yes to:

List of all the topics you would write about if you were writing books:

List of all the jobs you would work if every job paid the same:

List all the things you would do with one year of paid vacation:

List of all the things you need the most in this moment:

List of all the things you want the most in this moment:

_____
_____
_____
_____
_____
_____
_____
_____
_____
_____
_____
_____
_____
_____
_____
_____

List of all the beauty you've witnessed today:

List of everything you are good at and everything you are BEST at:

List the things people ask your help for:

List everything you enjoy doing on a day-to-day basis:

List of the things you do that you do NOT enjoy:

List of all the things you want to quit:

_____
_____
_____
_____
_____
_____
_____
_____
_____
_____
_____
_____
_____
_____
_____
_____
_____
_____
_____
_____

List of all the things you want to start:

List of all the things you want to finish:

List everything and everyone you are avoiding in your life:

List all the lies you tell yourself/beliefs about yourself that are holding you back:

List the lies you tell others:

List your excuses for not living your dreams:

List everything that you have left undecided:

List of everything you would create if you had a magic wand:

List everything you would make disappear if you had a magic wand:

List of everything you would change if you had a magic wand:

List of all your dreams:

List of all your fears:

List of everything you are going to do to start making your dreams a reality:

List of your own List of Lists:

MORE ROADMAPS

Alternative Worksheet #1

This is an alternative organizer to help you find clarity in areas you may feel stuck.

1. What areas of your life would you like to organize? In other words, where do you feel stuck?

_____
_____
_____
_____

2. Pick one area of your life that you would like to organize FIRST.

Area: _____

Things I want to let go of:

_____
_____
_____
_____

Things I'm afraid to let go of:

_____
_____
_____
_____

Things I want:

(The best-case scenario for this area of my life – dream scenario)

_____
_____
_____
_____
_____

3. What are you tolerating?

_____
_____
_____
_____
_____

4. List your SHOULDS versus your WANTS:

I should:	How I feel about it:	I want to:	How I feel about it:

5. What are your top three priorities for this area of life?

_____

_____

_____

_____

_____

In what ways, do you spend your time, energy, space, or money on things that are not aligned with your top priorities? In other words, how are you cluttering your life?

_____

_____

_____

_____

_____

6. List your Dreams:

_____

_____

_____

7. List your Fears:

_____

_____

_____

8. What is the first step you want to take?

_____

_____

_____

_____

_____

Alternative Worksheet #2

This is an alternative organizer to help you find clarity in areas you may feel stuck.

1. What area of your life would you like to organize the most? Why?

_____

_____

2. List the CLUTTER in your Life: (chose one area at a time)

Home:_____

_____

Work/Business:_____

_____

Relationships:_____

_____

Calendar (Time):_____

_____

Other:_____

_____

3. What are you TOLERATING?

_____

_____

_____

_____

4. List your SHOULDS versus your WANTS:

I should:	How I feel about it:	I want to:	How I feel about it:

5. What do you say "yes" to when you really want to say "no"?

_____

_____

_____

_____

_____

6. If you had a magic wand and could make any situation exactly the way you want it, what would it be? How would it be?

_____

_____

_____

_____

_____

7. Choose one thing that you want OR want to change. What is the first step you are going to take toward it?

_____
_____
_____
_____
_____

What obstacles (if any) are in the way of taking your first step?

_____
_____
_____
_____
_____
_____
_____
_____

How can you remove the obstacles or turn them into opportunities?

_____
_____
_____
_____
_____
_____

ABOUT THE AUTHOR

Christina Renzelli is a Transformational Coach who works with clients to create their ideal professional and personal lives. She guides her clients through transformations in business, careers, relationships, and life as they partner to clarify priorities, remove obstacles and limiting beliefs, and achieve success.

Christina began her professional career as an English language teacher overseas and continued her teaching career in the USA. After more than fifteen years of teaching and a life-altering experience, she decided to reinvent herself and help more people live truer to the goals and dreams they have been putting off in their own lives. Having previously created a business as a professional organizer in which she helped clients declutter their homes, she realized that her true passion has always been coaching and guiding individuals and organizations in creating greater structure and identifying opportunities to transform and excel. She believes that everyone has special talents, skills, and unique gifts to be shared with the world. She peels away the layers of her clients' stories with non-judgmental listening and truth-telling exploration so that they can hear the voice of their own wisdom, intuition and truth.

Christina Renzelli, M.Ed, ACC is an ICF Certified Coach. She received her coach training through the Core Essentials Program at Coach University, a Master's Degree in Teaching and Learning from DePaul University in Chicago, Illinois, and a Bachelor's Degree in Linguistics from Ohio University.

Made in the USA
Columbia, SC
28 August 2020